NOT ALOUD

NOT
ALOUD

CHRISTOPHER J. JARMICK

To Tim !
Enjoy !
Thanks

MoonPathPress

FIRST EDITION

Printed in the United States of America

ISBN: 978-1-936657-19-3

Cataloging Information: 1. Jarmick, Christopher J., 1958;
2. Contemporary American Poetry

Book design by Tonya Namura
using Baskerville

Cover art: When The Believers Try To Silence Their Gods
painted by Duane Kirby Jensen

Author photo, back cover: Timothy Aguero
Author photo, interior: Teresa Jarmick

MoonPath Press is dedicated to publishing the best poets of
the U.S. Pacific Northwest.

MoonPath Press
PO Box 1808
Kingston, Washington 98346

MoonPathPress@yahoo.com

http://MoonPathPress.com

For

Teresa,

my daughters:
Natasha, Natalia, Christina,

my parents:
Robert E. and Augusta

ACKNOWLEDGMENTS

Thanks are due to the following publishers/presses, magazines, journals, and newspapers who were first to publish some of the poems (or earlier versions of poems) that appear in *Not Aloud*, as follows: "600: A Poem About Baseball" *Poetry Quarterly* Spring 2015; "Dear Poem Owner" Poetry on Buses, King County Metro Transit and 4Culture 2014; "I Hate Peggy Lee" *Brutarian Magazine* 2004, *Poetry Quarterly* Summer 2015; "I Like Dead Poets: *Raven Chronicles*, Fall 2015; "My So Called American Life" *Real Change*, 2004; "Not a Poem About the Divorce" *Heart Splatters into Significance: Randomly Accessed Poetics Anthology*, Penhead Press, 2013; "Recovery Girl" *Here, There, Everywhere RASP Anthology*, 2013; "Today's Logic" *PoetsWest* Vol. V #3 2002; "Undeniably Seuss" *Many Trails to the Summit*, Rose Alley Press, 2010; "The Sky" *Poems for the Working Class*, 1983.

Special Thanks to David D. Horowitz of Rose Alley Press, who, beyond conversations, friendship and advice, offered his time and editing expertise, significantly improving more than 20 poems that appear in this collection. And of course to Lana Hechtman Ayers and MoonPath Press, whose efforts in assisting me to get this work out into the world was invaluable and gratefully appreciated.

Thanks to the many poetry hosts and organizers, specifically in Western Washington, whose notable efforts and time are often taken granted but who have greatly contributed to the vibrant Northwest Poetry community. Some of these people are: J. Glenn Evans, David D. Horowitz, Connie Walle, Garret Rutledge, Duane Kirby Jensen, Michael Dylan Welch, Lana Hechtman Ayers, Dobbie Reese Norris, Brendan McBreen, Gerald McBreen, Jerry and Pam Libstaff, Leopoldo Seguel, Jed

Meyers, Peter Monroe, Phoebe Bosche, Roy S. Seitz
and the late great Jack McCarthy. Also, organizations
like: The Olympia Poetry Network, Striped Water Poets
(of Auburn, WA), poetrynight (and Whatcom Poetry
Series of Bellingham), PoetsWest, Puget Sound Poetry
Connection, *Raven Chronicles*, Richard Hugo House,
LitFUSE, Watermark Poets, Jack Straw, 4 Culture and
the gone, but not forgotten Red Sky Poetry Theater and
Washington Poets Association WPA (whose efforts led to
the Burning Word Festival and Washington State having
a Poet Laureate). Thanks to independent book stores
like Park Place Books (owners Mary and Elizabeth) in
Kirkland, WA and Bookworm Exchange (owner Jim) in
Seattle, WA for allowing me to host poetry readings for
many years and supporting poetry with their generosity.

The cover, an original work of art *When The Believers
Try To Silence Their Gods* by Duane Kirby Jensen, adorns
the front of this book. When I saw the work in 2014, I
knew it HAD to be the cover of my book and fortunately
Duane made it possible for me to use it with his
permission and technical assistance. I'm lucky to have
such a great cover to go around my poems. Thank you,
thank you, thank you!

And thanks to the listeners, readers and lovers of poetry
who have reacted, commented, enjoyed, criticized and
opened your hearts and minds to my poetry scribblings
for so many years. You keep me writing, sharing and
hopefully improving every day I continue to breathe.

POETRY IS EVERYTHING

Poiesis (is the Greek root word for poetry that translates
literally 'to make' or create).

POEM
STARTER
#913

Hope is dissolved,
faith is compromised
when believers try to
silence their Gods.

for Duane

"You must stay drunk on writing so reality cannot destroy you."

—Ray Bradbury, *Zen in the Art of Writing*

CONTENTS

NOT A POEM

POLAROIDEUM

NOT ALOUD

NOT A POEM

"Poetry is the shadow cast by our streetlight imaginations."

—Lawrence Ferlinghetti

A Supermarket in Seattle

for Allen Ginsberg

I am full of thoughts of dead poets as I walk
by Lake Washington in a light drizzle,
staying under the trees.

The weather is getting worse
so I head toward the co-op grocery,
looking forward to the hot latte
I will treat myself to.
I wave to Doctor Williams
out for his late afternoon walk.

As I enter glass doors into a fluorescent
wash-out of natural color,
I imagine a poem called
"The Howling Song of My Lorax Wasteland."
What images I conjure!

A weeping willow crying red tears;
an obscene pile of twisted car metal
wraps around its trunk.

It should be a Dalí painting hung above
where the local neighborhood newspapers
and real estate rental magazines gather.

As I stalk past the not-so-wild asparagus
and hairy coconuts,
I spy Babies snorting spilled coffee grinds, and
husbands nonchalantly making
a feminine hygiene product selection
before rushing to cold beer refrigerator.

Out of the corner of my eye
      I spy Allen Ginsberg playing grab ass
            with the white bearded Walt Whitman.

They scurry around the corner and
I wonder what mischief they are up to.
I am distracted
            by movement
around the red roma tomato bins.
It is a brightly colored bird,
perhaps Mayzie herself,
on vacation while poor Horton
keeps her egg warm.

A well-dressed formal man orders
tea from the small coffee counter.
                  What is Eliot doing in Seattle?
It seems he's not being understood.
                  Perhaps I can help.
I quickly maneuver to order my latte,
            but Eliot has vanished.
I see a hand beckoning me from down the aisle—
attached are finger cymbals.
I know it must be Ginsberg.

America, oh America, what time and space
continuum has been disturbed
so the ghosts of past poets descend
upon this supermarket of Seattle?

I am not mad!
So what?
Inspiration?

What lesson?
What purpose does it serve to show me the old men
and show them to me now,
years after I would be beyond impressed with such stunt?

A crash!
Vinegar bottles have been broken on Aisle 12!
Hundreds of brussel sprouts are rolling down Aisle 4
toward the large lady as she reaches for
a super-size bag of fat-free chips!

I see the man in the long straggly
gray beard leave the store;
I must follow.

They roam the earth, disturbing the vegetables
in supermarkets.

Where do we roam now father Ginsberg,
grandfather Whitman,
Uncle Eliot?

Cousin Geisel blurts out a rhyme:
"Why for goodness sake,
haven't you been paying attention?
We meet with Blake.
With Blake we meet;
in the garden section
at Home Depot.
He'll have a rake.
Blake with rake
awaits."

I hesitate.

Not a Poem That Rhymes

We do not want the poems that rhyme.
We do not want them any time.
We are so sick of rhyming verse,
poems of love are even worse.

If you send us rhyming poem,
we'll return it to its home.
Into white envelope with much haste
or if no stamp, then in the waste.

If you want to be in print,
then kindly take our little hint.
We do not want the poems that rhyme.
We not want them any time.

Oh but surely you can see
what rhyming poems mean to me,
how their cadences rise and fall
creating them keeps me tall.

I love the poems that rhyme.
I love them most, all the time.
And I worked so hard to write them down,
your rejections make me frown.

You think the poems with rhyming,
have quaint annoying timing.
Scribbled by quaint old nerds,
clutching too tight their precious words.

The rhyming poems may be old school,
but not all come from older fool.
The rules on rhyme poems that you make
I must violate, I must break.

I'm not too old, nor much too thin.
I do not have pale pasty skin.
I like Rexroth, Whitman, Sexton too,
but no rhymes ever, would make me blue.

It's rhyming poems I want to see.
Sing song ditties created by me.
They must dissolve your dirty look,
get published in your brand new book.

Poem Starter #1,713

Every 7
(Not 13 or 17) years
cicadas seem
to invade
the poetry I read
showing up in several poems
published in *The Atlantic*
and *Poetry Magazine*.

My All-Controlling Muse

with apologies to Carolyn Kizer

The moment I start to read poetry
I am compelled to immediately
start writing one of my own.
My jealous muse believes
if I'm thinking of poetry I should not waste any time
on another's but get to work creating my own.

Let me apologize this day to Carolyn Kizer.
My muse rudely interrupted
my moment with **the great blue heron**,
(*"Heron whose ghost are you?"*),
perhaps my favorite Kizer poem.

But I was not able to savor the words,
nor bask in the imagery, this morning,
NO.
For as soon as I started to read,
my muse cleared her throat, elbowed my gut,
blew in my ear,
and demanded I start writing my own.

The other day it happened when I tried to read
some poems from *What I Saw* by Jack McCarthy.
And before that it was Lawrence Ferlinghetti's
Endless Life collection. This morning
I just wanted fifteen minutes
with Carolyn Kizer's *Mermaids in the Basement*,
but it was not to be.

My muse is a jealous bitch,
selfish to a fault.

11

I try not to give in to the impatiently mean queen,
but no technique will thwart her.
She is more stubborn than even I at my most ornery.
So THIS, then, is the work of HER insistence!
Perhaps she will see what an awful poem
has been created because of her rude demand,
perhaps your disapproval will dissuade
her future attempts
to be so all controlling
when I try to read a few poems
by someone I admire.

Alas, I fear this won't be the case,
she has no patience and hates it so
when another's poem steals her light
and shares our private space.

Poem Starter #25 or 6 Two 4

The best thing about not writing hit songs
is you don't have to sing them over
and over
and over
again.

Poem Starter #1,409

The music of language
minus the overture
guitar, flute, drum solo
or over-dubs
is poetry.

Holler for the Blues King

"The blues was bleeding the same blood as me."

—B.B. King

1.

From holding the reins of a mule,
pulling a hoe through Mississippi cotton fields,
hearing the "field holler" lament sung by
a single voice in a minor scale
to watchin' daylight through
the spaces 'tween walls of
a single room shack,
and wide eyed glances
through outside slats
into the Ebony Club watching couples
jitterbuggin, snake-hipping, ch'choo boogie
and trucking.

From church gospel to Blind Lemon blues,
to watchin' Bukka play slide on a piece o' pipe
producing tremolo sounds that moved through
your insides, makin' the peach fuzz hairs
on your arms dance and tickle your skin.
From trickin' stupid fingers that wouldn't slide
into slick swivel of wrist from elbow
back and forth, stretchin' the string,
raisin' and lowering the pitch of the note,
while other fingers stretch out—
a fluttering gesture,
butterflies flapping their wings.

2.

From singing dialogues with guitar
to melding counter melodies,
one passionate note to another,
to learning craft techniques from
Memphis Handy Park musicians.

Radio D J Beale Blues Boy to B. B.
Chitlin' circuit juke joints to Carnegie Hall.
Witnessing castration and lynching,
bombs exploding in hotels shared
with Martin Luther King.

In every obbligato
tribute to Blues pioneers,
that rich signature sound—
horns, bass, drums, guitar and
his beloved Lucille.

I Hate Peggy Lee

I hate Peggy Lee.

I hate her for that song she did,
you know which one I mean.

The one where she talks
through part of it
and then sings about
dancing and booze
in a voice that tells you
she did a lot of living,
backed with that
damn banjo.

It's a great song,
perhaps one of the best there ever was.
Jerry Leiber and Mike Stoller
wrote a timeless classic,
but I wish 'em horrible deaths
for making that cursed song.

You start thinking about
what you done with your life…
and whether it seems like you done a lot
or you done nothin', you think…

So you get smart about things and decide,
it don't do you any good
thinking about things like that—
just depresses you, brings you down
and there's already plenty of things
to be down about

without letting what belongs to someone else
add another level of funk.
So you turn it off,
you don't think about it
you never play the song
and you just pretend it never existed.

That's a fine strategy but then,
you'll hear someone else say the phrase,
or you'll hear the song on someone's radio,
or on a jukebox
or someone's whistling the tune.

Not your fault,
but it's back in your head again.

You're watching a really good TV show,
a movie everyone calls a classic,
or you read a great book
and as you get to the end of it
you say,
"okay that was good,
but...'

Sometimes you're okay
with it.
I mean fuck it,
so what,
who said there had to be anything more,
than what it is.
You smile at the irony,
and that makes it all right.

But it's not.
It is not alright at all.
Not really.
You come back to it.
Come back to it
over and over again.
You see some sports player
do the most spectacular thing
or some guy on the Olympics
makes a new world's record
or you just had the best sex
you ever had in your life,
or you just laughed so hard
it made your eyes water.. .

You can be feeling as low
as any man ever felt
or be feeling so good
you wonder how it will
ever get any better…
and then you hear it,
right before you go to sleep
or when you're standing,
just standing
watching a spectacular sunset
with a double rainbow
and sun beams breaking
through cotton ball clouds,
shimmering off some
tranquil azure blue
body of water…

and then all you can hear
in your head
is Peggy Lee's question.

Small Circle of Brautigan

or *Not a Poem About Critics*

If you won't arrest me
I will throw a rock through the window
of the asylum.

No, wait! If I throw a rock
through the window of the asylum,
you will think I'm crazy
and have me committed.

I need to do something wrong
and make sure I am caught.
When you ask me why
 I threw the rock, I must reply:
"I don't know why I threw the rock
through the window,
I just felt like it and didn't think
you would catch me."
If I tell you I did it because
I wanted to be arrested,
you will have me committed.

I am already committed
which is why I want to be arrested.
It's the only way to escape the freedom
that has given me more
responsibility than I asked for.

I don't remember if I asked to be born or not.
Most of us are too young to remember
what it was
we said in the womb of our mothers.
I can't trust my parents to tell me
the truth about this,
they only hear what they want to hear.
I don't know if they listened better
then or now.

I do know I never asked to grow up.

I want to be arrested because
I will never be able
to share my poems
with Richard Brautigan.
He stopped writing too long ago
and he won't be able to remind me
criticism doesn't matter at all.

Poem Starter #1,224

If you aren't famous
you never HAVE
to dress up.

Big Dots

Flo and Eddie
walked into a bar
and Dick Dale
showed 'em a surf guitar
riff,
but they knew they had to
get to Pomona.
It was a dream they had.

"Look," the waitress winked,
"I've got some new shag carpet at my place
that needs to be broken in."
She was ahead of her time.

I knew there was no place I would rather be…
No, wait—
there was one other place!
I needed to get there.

The top was down on my car again
and I raced along Pacific Coast Highway,
at that perfect mid-60s point in time
(you know the intersection).

I pulled over at Zuma and saw the girl
with the polka dot bikini.
I floated across the sand to her
and could not have been more smooth
if I was peanut butter
on the roof
of Annette Funicello's mouth.

I might have been.

Anyway,
I became the dots…
for a while.

Pollocked Out

Flawed brush stroke of blue
on white thick textured paper.
A flick of camel hair brush
discarded by artist gone mad.
Drip by paint drip.
Perhaps the fumes,
perhaps never knowing.
Good enough? Fake?
Fabulously famous,
intensified doubts,
crippling depression.
Who can you trust?

The liquor lit his belly on fire,
spun the room so fast,
laughing out cries.
Collapsed without caring,
the anger released,
the self-loathing too.
An artist has no rules.
Take a too young lover,
drive when drunk,
shit in your pants.
It's what is expected.

The secret to living forever
is to make sure you die too young,
so a few can get rich
off your rage.

Poem Starter #1,429

The sound of nothing
wasn't heard,
but the meaningless
of the moment

mattered.

Today's Logic

I squint my eyes and imagine everything
looking like a wet watercolor painting
dripping color, de-forming and bending
in ways that Dalí himself never tried.

I was thinking of making that
the title of the poem
but that was several minutes ago.

I was staring into the ozone
lost in a head-on collision of thoughts
that vaporized upon focus,
and then my cell phone
rang.

It was John Ashcroft.
He wanted me to tell him about the guy
sitting at the next table
and what kind of Denny's
breakfast special
he was ordering.
"You might be able to tell
he's a terrorist
from what he orders,"
he said quickly.
I knew better than to argue—
Republican logic
it's simply impenetrable.
I told Ashcroft he should worry
about the guy in the parking lot instead

or what the new flavor at
Baskin Robbins is this month
and hung up.

Wait a minute I thought,
this isn't Denny's.

Poem Starter #2,013

The definition of insanity
is repeating the same thing
over and over and over again:
"Guns Don't Kill People... "

The definition of insanity is
Guns Don't Kill People.

My So-Called American Life

You've programmed me to want more
than I can afford.
Taught me to be able to get more
than I can afford.
So I can owe someone more
than I can afford,
for the rest of my unnaturally
extended life.

I am one big never-ending
Oliver Stone movie.
I am a giant mouth with an insatiable
sweet tooth and unquenchable thirst.
My rush needs a rush.
I need to shout, scream
AND yell at 11 in 12 speaker
surround sound that I deserve

More! More! More!!!

Inject 1000 ccs of distraction into
my pulmonary artery
so I can permanently escape from reality.
Let me recapture my forgotten spent youth,
own ALL the songs I ever got high to in college.

Gimme the movies I first saw in between commercials, in black and white. Monty Hall's Castro convertible couch, A NEW CAR, a modern ALL ELECTRIC house with antique dining room chair replicas made of indestructible polyurethane plastic that don't squeak. I want my kids to have EVERYTHING they want as long as I give it to them, and they know that I gave it to them, and they tell all their friends that I gave it to them AND they love for me for it even...

More! More! More!!!

I deserve it!
I think hard, wish hard, play hard.
Paying the interest ON the interest,
I master the credit card roulette.
I'm the re-finance king, robbing Peter
to pay Paul AND Mary.
I don't have to pay for half of it
until the next decade.

I want to invent a new sense
so I can over-stimulate it,
plug it into the internet
and let it fly and crash through
game sites, sex sites, chat rooms until
I wind up a flashing pop up
SPAM ad on a billion screens.

I've given up on religion and politics.
No time to think. Everyone I know is crooked,
telling me too LOUDLY
what they think I want to hear.
I can't take it with me,
so I better enjoy it all, right now.
I'm steering my car with my knees
so I can text:

More! More! More!!!

Crash landing on a mold-infested bad lollipop cruise ship
I realize everything I've enjoyed has made me fat, sick,
lazy and dumber than the Hollywood suits who approved
the blockbusters I watch on my personal two-story 3-D
IMAX home theatre. So make me forget and strap me
into the roller coaster ride and go faster. No pain, all gain.

Give me:
the recycled, updated brand new, all improved, retro,
advanced, new age, stunning technological breakthrough,
with added bells, whistles, extended warranty, money back
guarantee, free servicing and updating for life. Let me
swallow the latest pill that makes me stay up two inches
younger and thinner. I'll drink it down with a triple shot,
mocha, almond mint, all fat, tall, sprinkle of cinnamon,
with room for

More! More! More!!!

Poem Starter #86

The poetry of drunks
is sobering.

Recovery Girl

for Daria

Recovery Girl
takes her first few steps
on the tight-rope
stretched over
relapse canyon.

Loved ones
hold their breath for her
needing to help,
knowing they must not.

There's little confidence
inside Recovery Girl.

She must trust words
from an invisible coach,
ignore how naked
how utterly alone she feels.
And she must fight
with every thread of her soul
that irresistible urge
to look down.

Poem Starter #119

Poets

S
o
M
e
T
I
M
e
S

a   s   s   i   s   t

oth

ers

to C

things

.yltnereffid

Not a Bowl Full of Cherries

I've had a revelation
that life is like
a cup full of noodles.

Not just any cup o' noodles
but Maruchan Instant Lunch:
chicken flavored, caution HOT.

Hot, cup of bland broth,
cardboard-tasting ramen noodles,
twelve dehydrated corn kernels,
nine carrot slivers
and eight peas.

Hot cup of MSG broth
causes dull headache,
like nine-to-five job.

Styrofoam cup of quick
caloric intake—salty.
I have a method.

A method to tease
with three spoonfuls
of plain noodles and broth.

And then to please
with a bite that includes:
O glorious, flavorful
sweet pea !!!!

Conservatively save sweet pea,
only eight,
the spark of life in bland salty broth

Life is like a cup
of dehydrated Insta-lunch.

More peas please !!!

Word Tripping

One moment I was free associating
in a stream of consciousness
kind of a way,
and the next I stumbled upon
a word that stuck up in my path,
tripped me,
and caused me to fall face first
into a pile of mildewed adverbs.

Lazy bunch those adverbs!
Too lazy to move around or even shower,
but I realized no one had picked one up
or dusted one off for a while.

While trying not to inhale,
I said, "You know people
might like you better
if you didn't smell so bad."
"Maybe it's you who smell bad,"
Merrily said.
"Who said we wanted to be liked,"
Lovingly said quickly.
"Who asked for your opinion,"
Snappily added carefully.

I got up, dusted myself off,
flicked off an extra l-y
(that was clinging onto a loose thread
in my jacket),
and continued on my way.
I was careful to walk all the way around
the puddle of clichés

and would have gotten here on time
if I didn't slip on some puns
as I tried to use a short cut
around the valley of pronouns.
I wound up at the Word Fair.
They had a sale on words
that rhyme with you.
I spent a few minutes
looking through the Just-the-Right-Word bin,
but they were out of the one I really wanted.

Ah well, at least I resisted
the urge to buy
a pocket of old sayings.

The Hackerfocky

with apologies to Lewis Caroll

'Twas google and the oldsy yahoo
    Did yawn and twitter on the net
All vixens were the babyboos
    And our lilt crocks confet

Beware the Hackerfock, my son
    With pics that lie, posts that kill
Beware the cyber bull, Facebook shun
    The criminy slackerwill

He took his fermal mouse in hand
    Long search for nerdist foe he scoured
Distracted he, by EBAY ads
    YouTube cats devoured

And, in his unprotected viewing
    The Hackerfock with tools of shame
Attacked with virus spewing
    And IM'd as it came

The fermal mouse went clickity click
    Zero, one, Zero, one, track and track
He quarantined and took its head
    message-boarding frack

And hast thy newbie slain Hackerfock?
    Emoticoms, to you dear boy,
Oh yangpo day! Vacroo! Bishay!
    They gleetexted in their joy

'Twas google and the oldsy yahoo
  Did yawn and twitter on the net
All vixens were the babyboos
  And our lilt crocks confet

Undeniably Seuss

an homage to the most influential poet of the modern age

Oh the places I would go,
and the things I could do,
and all the thinks I
could think
just to gaze upon your
sneetches,
smell your
green eggs and ham
or to touch your
Yertle.

My mouth waters
when I think of
your Ying
or you and the Gox
with the yellow socks -
that mop noodled finch.
Oh what I would do with
your Nazzim of Bazim,
if given half a chance.

Nothing
can prevent
this obsession I have,
not Bipper or Skipper or Dinwoodie
Slinky, Stinky or any of the other
Fuddnudler Brothers,
not the single-file Zumzian Zuks,
the south-going Zax,
Thidwick the Moose,
the quick Queen of Quincy

or even the Mayor of Who-ville himself
can control
this Zizzer zazzer zuss of a wocket
I feel that surpasses my longing
for Little Lola Lopp
or the Right Side up Song Girls
or even Yolanda Waldo Yorenson.

Now don't get all
Miss Fuddle-dee Duddle
on me,
or tell me I'm no better
than a Peeping Nerkle,
or I belong with
Van Vleck the Vipper of Vipp.

Horton the Elephant
and the Mayzie Bird
told me in no Kweet,
Kwigger or Klots
that
my Preep Pelf Proo
was made for your
Sneelock,
and you can count
your Zummers
that I won't be denied.

I'll count one fish
two fish
red fish
blue fish
win the Butter Battles,
and cooperate
with Sam I am,
but I'll hold
your vrooms,
caress your
Yertles,
And walk
Wumbus in Woomp
with you down
Mulberry Street
if it's the very very last
thing I
ever Terwilliger do.

Poem Starter #1,315

Sometimes a
blank page
is just
a blank page
and sometimes it is better off staying
a blank page.

Poem Starter #1,207

There is mostly white blank

space

around these words,

silence

defined by its invader.

POLAROIDEUM

"If you do not breathe through writing,
if you do not cry out in writing,
or sing in writing,
then don't write,
because our culture has no use for it."

—Anaïs Nin

Poem Starter #1,958

Listen closely
and you'll hear the sound
of my life
beating.

That Was the Sound

I said:

That was the sound of ironic laughter hitting the trees
that no one heard in the forest of hidden tears,
beyond the land of hope and dreams, at the end of
rainbow pot of gold good intentions wasted on
spoiled apathetic Argonauts, haunted by
a golden fleece and 1001 nights of Eros,
now on an ark for forty days and forty nights
with starving animals plotting mutiny.

I said:

That was the sound of a teardrop sliding down
smooth olive skin, falling towards the ground
creating breeze of melancholy before it splashes
into a flood of forgotten memories that taste
more bitter than all the war dead of the Germans
whose family wondered what they died for
as they sweep dirt from kitchen floors, warm
with ovens baking strudels for tourists, who
are on too tight a schedule to
touch Dresden art.

I said:

That was the sound of madness screaming
quietly inside a skull shell protecting the syrup
of broken vows, promises and dreams that explodes
into sharp shards of penetrating stares dispensed by
disapproving uniformed elders shaking bony fingers
at huge purple Irises being overly sensual in a world of
reactionary stimuli that slithers silently up on you
until you laugh.

Listen.

Wind Chill

As I unscrew the top of my head
there's enough hollow space inside
it sounds like I'm taking the cap off
a mason jar of blueberry preserves.
I say blueberry but I'm thinking
sour cherry—
so tart your mouth puckers and your eyes water.
I should probably cry.
It's been too long.

"Crazy," she would say,
but, I don't tell her these things anymore.
The aluminum wind chimes gently ting-inging,
hearing the breeze through trees,
around uneven spaces of roof and gutter.
I fly over the lake, a cool gray
reflecting the cloudy winter sky.
The air is making the skin on my face
feel like cellophane.
(I write cellophane not because
it's one of those words
used too many times by poets in the 1980s,
but because my face
really did feel like cellophane).

"It's going," I answer into the phone.
"I'm on the deck."
I haven't seen her face in a long time
and wonder how her hair looks now.

There was once a hot humid summer
a couple had found their dream home
"too good to be true."

"What are you thinking about?" she asked.

"Our house," I said.

There was silence.

Key

We stand watching the little piles of bones
the dog never buried.
She wanted me to see this
and understand.

I nod my head
I am ready,
perhaps.

We walk out through the woods,
back onto the path
over the running creek, wide enough
we have to jump to the other side,
scramble up an embankment
and into the tool shed
where I notice on the work bench
a hip bone.

I look at her.
She smiles.
It's important that I understand.

She takes out a small box
covered in dust
opens it with a key.
She takes out a velvet cloth.
Slowly she reveals
a handle to a kitchen drawer,
scorched from a fire.

She wants me to remember.

The Sky

The sky
is easy to take for granted
You almost don't see how quickly it changes
... like you.

The clouds
are not metaphors at all.
They hide the sky,
they get fat,
sometimes they burst,
but not with tears,
Mr. Tambourine Man,
just with rain

Now rain
can wash you clean,
but there are better
more modern,
more practical ways
to get the surface of things
clean.

The sky
doesn't hold anything.
It's not a canvas.

Sky
doesn't hold anything,
not my hand,
not my dreams,
...anymore.

Sky
can't remember a thing,

but
I can.

Poem Starter #1,912

We listen,
often without hearing,
handy for TV commercials,
bad for spouses
and poetry.

Not A Break-up Poem

Blood on the dishes
in the sink.
It's part of the pattern,
but we didn't
realize
until
too late.

Spots on the glasses.
You insist
they shouldn't
be there.
I think they add
character.

The knives are
dull,
don't cut right.
They won't sharpen
but I don't
want to buy new ones,
not yet ready to throw them
out.

Faucets
leak.

After we washed
the brand new Egyptian
high thread count silk sheets,
we noticed
the discoloration.

Reminds me of blood
on the dishes
in the sink.

Too late.
It's part of the pattern.

Poem Starter #1,526

Yesterday,
words in my
writer's box
were screaming.

I punished them
by not writing them down.

Not A Poem About the Divorce

Signing the declaration
of dependence,
on the yacht
left in the desert,
we sailed to the
land of 50 percent off—
thanks to solar powered windmills,
but inventory was shrinking so fast.

We couldn't tie the
boat to the dock,
so we saw the
end of the world
and laughed when the bananas
slipped on the human skeletons.

Then she says she doesn't
"understand me anymore."

I told her to jump,
but she got a lawyer
and we split everything
in half.

I tried to tell her getting even,
means you haven't gained a thing.
She didn't listen,
she never listened.
So the boat sank
and we fell into the water.

"See, you're no good
without me,"
she screamed.

I didn't actually hear
her say this;
we were drowning at
the time.

Poem Starter: The Movie

Three movie quotes
walk into a bar:

first one says:
"Pain don't hurt."

second one says:
"Gentlemen, you can't fight in here,
this is the war room."

third one says:
"Shut the fuck up, Donny."

Bleak

The rest of your life will consist of
depriving yourself of most pleasures,

compromising your strongest beliefs,
giving up many of your dreams,

eating and drinking far less then you desire
so you can live longer,
participate in uncomfortable
social settings,
which pass the time
so you don't think too much about

the aches and pains of your rotting body,
that itch you can't scratch,
that lost moment you can't forget,
and that regret you refuse to bury.

You tell yourself there is pleasure
in chores, in accepting responsibility
in giving to others what you never had,
in raising children to emulate
acceptable behaviors.

You believe rewards are present in the doing,
in the journey and in an after-life
you have faith exists.

You are in fear of almost everything
and haunted by your thoughts
every waking hour.

You escape through a maze
of unbelievable truths,
faith and self-delusions.

You realize it's best
not to think

bleak.

The Cost of Everything

I turn right,
at the corner
and as I do a blue truck speeds
through the stop sign
hitting the red car
that turned left,
that should have been me.
Should I believe
my fickle faith in God
is perhaps the reason
I was spared?

The part that really happened
could have been much worse.
But when I ask 'why me?'
There is no answer…

I turned right, by mistake,
I needed to turn left, but I was lost in thought
and singing *Baker Street*
from memory.
If I had turned left
I would have been hit by blue truck.

Am I then responsible for the red car's fate?
As I heard the horrible sound,
looked in my rear view mirror,
saw what had happened,
should I have stopped?
Should I have told the police
it should have been me?
I needed to turn left, but I turned right,

because my mind was lost,
remembering how I used to sing
along to Gerry Rafferty and the song
Baker Street
back when I pretended to suffer
in a dull relationship,
rotting away north of Los Angeles
miles from the dream
of making movies in Hollywood,
thousands of miles away from
where I was born.

Maybe I should keep driving.
Maybe this is the way I am told
it is time to go.
I turned the wrong way,
but it was the sign
I should leave everything behind.

The different life I made,
the family I was part of,
the new dreams I had,
was this my last chance
to get somewhere else?
Was the devil behind me?

Can the officer give me a ticket
for reckless abandonment of fate?
"You're responsible for this accident
because it should have been you."
Or maybe he'd declare:
"God may have blessed you, today,
but the law is not superstitious,

the law is very clear
and you will pay for what you did…
Now feet apart, hands behind your back
…I'm taking you in!"

I stop staring at the over-sized
television screen
in the appliance store.
I don't need this.
I can wait to buy this.

As I back away from plasma screens
I envision in my Jetson-style penthouse
over-looking the coastal waters
of pastel painted sunset perfection,
a salesman in a clean dark blue suit
(I almost bought at 50 percent off
a few weeks ago) says:
"Can I answer any questions for you?"
I shake my head, "Not today."

I've resisted the temptation,
stayed strong,
so I decide it is okay to reward myself,
but they do not have a copy of
City to City on CD
I consider *Best of Steelers Wheel*
with the song "Stuck in the Middle of You,"
and I almost let myself have it,
but no,
it is *Baker Street*

I need and want,
and they don't have it on any CDs.
Time to go.

In the parking lot,
a child recklessly runs, laughing,
away from his parents.
I hear the squeal of rubber
as a car stops too fast.

I freeze.

I look toward the sound
hoping the parents will not have to pay
with years of guilt and sorrow
for a moment of inattention
to their child,
hoping my avoiding a near accident
an hour ago
hasn't somehow created this one.

I hear the "Oh my God" of the mother,
and then the father's gruff scolding voice,
"Hold my hand in the parking lot!"

No one gets hurt today.

Cue the saxophone.

Homestead

Yesterday,

the nearly 50 year old
house

my 87 year old
parents

lived in
was listed for sale.

Nearly 3,000
miles away,

I picture its rooms full of
things.

I picture its rooms
empty

silently awaiting new
possessions.

House Story

"Everyone loves a story.
Let's begin with a house."
—Phillip Levine

The house
filled with things
in precise places
—for comfort, for show.

Front room with plastic couches ready for guests
who never came. Children forbidden to play
here.

Grey rug shows imprint of china cabinet
displaying fancy plates
and hand-painted porcelain music boxes,
few ever touched.
There was no clutter, no living done here.

There is the kitchen and here is the stove
which held big cast-iron frying pans
and giant pots for soup.
A silver fan above,
still there under dark brown grease
to transport into sky,
smoke, steam and cooking smells.

Laminate counter where dishes stacked,
scratched, stained and cracked.
Once washed of evidence, they couldn't hint
of what they once held, not unlike an empty page—

waiting for drawings, notes or stories needing telling
of the family in this place.
                    Look
                    there:
the door moldings dented where kitchen table hit
then turned and maneuvered to pass on through,
placed in position with anticipation,
moved out in bitter haste.

"Sit up straight." "Your turn to clean the table."
"His night to wash the plates." Mom and Dad laughing,
then not speaking at all except: "elbows off the table."
An empty seat on occasion barely considered
but vacated chair for longer
added chill into the air.

On top of that stained linoleum
was a once-prized cooler.
Laughter, celebration, the day it was delivered—
magic—it automatically defrosted.

Beyond the fence in back,
the woods and running creek
tadpoles, crawdads, turtles,
crickets and sometimes snakes.
Wild pheasants, deer, rumors of a bear.
But over-time the crowded trees came down.
New neighbors, lawns, more fences, pools.
Where did Dad go and then the rest?
Do you really have to ask?

Hear the Saturday morning mowers echo,
sizzling barbecues in summer.
Remember: burnt hotdogs in the air,
tag, little league, flag football—laughter.
Before the year, winter followed spring.

Now, just empty shells,
scars barely faded.

Poem Starter #1,315

If I write hard enough
and the pencil point doesn't break,
the paper doesn't tear,
or the keyboard doesn't crack,
then maybe…maybe
I'll no longer hear the door slamming,
or breaking of the glass.

Polaroid 5

My cousin runs in mock terror as I insist on kissing her
in the way children will play.
We ping pong,
shake our heads at the antics
of uncles and aunts who seem sillier than we.

Grandfather boogie-woogies at the piano
his childish hands rag timing and dancing on the keys
syncopating into a march, as he makes exaggerated faces
then as he shifts gears into a soothing classical lullaby
and adults gather for his show,
we run outside to play tag.

When the air gets cooler, the light grows dim,
we realize time has not stood still,
not even for us,
who were having such fun.
We all insist on coming through the door at once
and several of us pop inside.

We enjoy slices of turkey and vegetables
too young
to appreciate each detail,
instead it is the warmth, the noise, the mood
and wondering when the ice cream
with hot fudge will appear.

I am years away from ever thinking to reach back
and recapture these moments in words
of grandma's large house,
the family gathering
that influences and lingers
long after the details I never knew well
fade...

like memories and lives
are supposed to do.

New Suit

New suit:
1965.

New suit:
Palm Sunday.

New suit:
Robert Hall.

New suit:
for Easter.

New suit:
to wear Sundays.

New suit:
for little man.

New suit:
blonde hair.

New suit:
special day.

New suit:
Communion.

New suit:
next Easter.

New Suit:
Confirmation.

New Suit:
cousin's wedding.

New suit
Palm Sunday again.

New suit:
Aunt's funeral.

New suit:
green plaid.

New suit.

Dad insists on
new suit.

Don't like
new suit.

To hell with
new suit.

So....no
new suit
for me.

Polaroid 6

Sliding down hillsides of snow
on book bags
we yell.

But it doesn't feel as much fun
as last year.

More interesting is watching the old man
at the counter, with grimy fingers,
smoking cigarette scraps,
never quite clearing his throat
despite all the noise,
adding something to the soda
on the counter
from a bottle in paper bag from his pocket.

What mysterious potion
does he possess?

Poem Starter #1,530

They say
Man has no natural predator.

We do,
however,
have each other.

My Favorite Nightmare

Trapped in a dark cave,
so terrified, breath
sucks into my open mouth,
My eyes wide—just enough light to see
gigantic monstrous fingers reaching
closer,
closer.

There is no place to run. No place to hide.

A finger larger than my arm,
brushes against my shirt.
Sharp fingernail scratches through
the material against my chest
slips into my pocket.

I press my left shoulder against
cool rock of the dark cave.
The giant's fingertip bigger than
my fist pulls at my pocket.
His chainsaw growl
echoes in the cavern.

"No… no… no…" I tremble.
Threads in my pocket tear.
I plant my feet firm on the ground
push away from the giant,
my back against the cold damp cave wall,
I'm just a boy—I don't want to die.

The pocket tears away
the giant's arm lunges,
stretches just enough
so that fingers clutch hold
of my shirt.
The giant roars,
he pulls.

My feet slide and scrape on the dirt.
I am being dragged closer to giant.
"STOP!"I gasp.
Wake up!
 "NO!"

My recurring nightmare as a child,
a combination of real life
and an old 1950s monster movie.
My sweat, rapid breath indicate my fear,
but I smile, an almost rapture
warms from within.
It was after all
just a nightmare—
my favorite nightmare.
The one I've had many times before
though not in a very long time.

And the nightmare reminded me
as a 7 year old boy I hid
in the very back of a deep closet.
Safe, I heard muffled voices outside,
and drifted off to sleep.
Hours later, when I appeared in front

of my mother in the kitchen
she gasped, dropped silverware
on the floor and then…
"Thank God,"
hugging me tight.
She had been worried.
I had disappeared,
everyone was looking for me.
No one knew I fell asleep in the closet.

And the nightmare reminded me
of resting my head on grandma's arm,
watching scary movie on black and white TV.
A young couple scared, trapped in a cave,
as the monster moves closer,
knowing the couple is inside.
Nana was more scared than me.
"Are you sure we should watch this?"
"Yes, this is good."
"This is horrible, very scary," she said.
"You'll get nightmares…I'll get nightmares…."
"It's only a movie, Nana,
only a movie, don't be scared."
The Giant Cyclops reaches into
the small cave opening,
the young couple cower against the back wall,
waving a torch at the giant hand.

As my eyes opened,
ending my favorite nightmare,
I knew my mom and Nana loved me.
I remember the boy
the nightmares,
and when I first discovered
and began to understand
pure, unconditional love.

Polaroid 7

The teacher refused to teach,
ignoring my question
failing to explain,
worse than school mate taunt,
than even a spanking.
I feel embarrassed,
become invisible.

At night Father yells:
"You're lazy!
You are stupid!"

I cry without tears
not knowing what to do.
Powerless,
I yell back in silence.

Near bed time
my cat contentedly purrs
because I pet him.

Jealously, I stop.

Not A Poem About High School

Spackenkill High, Poughkeepsie, New York

This poem is certainly not one about high school
(that is the last thing I would write about).
So this poem is not about high school—
(it's not).

The jocks, the heads, the brains, the class clowns,
the rejects, the black kids,
the Asians, the new kids,
the babes, the cheap dates, the juvies,
the retards and the invisible ones.

The rich, the poor, the upper middle class
and the ones we knew nothing about,
but we heard things.
The polite, the goofy, the hairy before their time,
the virgins, the promiscuous,
the perverted, the beautiful, the handsome,
The polite, the rude, the ugly,
the carpenters daughters, the fat slobs
and the one with cancer.

The people who ignored me,
the people who watched my back,
the people who betrayed me,
the people who picked on me.
The people I admired, the people
I fantasized about touching,
the people whose lives I wanted,
the people who I felt sorry for,
and the people I thought about killing
…slowly.

The embarrassing moments,
the acts of cruelty, aggression,
and teenagism and the times
too horrible or just far too
dull to remember.

This poem is certainly not one about high school
(that is the last thing I would write about).
So this poem is not about high school
(it's not).

Subliminal Messages

I knew *Kukla* and *Ollie* were cheap sock puppets
but quite frankly
there was something very strange and creepy
about Fran.
She seemed too needy. They were always too safe
and I know they would never show me or tell
me anything I wasn't supposed to know.

Lamb Chop was much more than a puppet
and Shari Lewis was someone I wanted to meet.
Occasionally, things seemed to get completely out-of-hand
but I knew if I paid very close attention
they would whisper something important to me.

Sometimes I thought *Davey* and *Goliath* were
going to do something truly awful to *Gumby* and *Pokey*.
I wasn't quite jaded enough to figure out what it might be
at 6
but before I was 11, I knew.

I recognized my life was not going to be easy when
The Soupy Sales Show was cancelled.
I still think "Pachalafaka" is romantic
and I can dance the "Mouse."
Soupy pretended the show was for very little kids,
but he talked and played to the older souls
adults forget that kids have.
That was why they had to take the show away.

Sonny Fox quit *Wonderama*
and when squeaky clean Bob McCallister took over
it became *Kids are People Too.*
That was much too patronizing for me.
I was glad for Sandy Becker, Art Linkletter and Chuck
    McCann.

Captain Kangaroo was a little darker
and more unpredictable
than *Mr. Rogers.*
I guess I favor Bob slightly over Fred.
Fred never seemed to be in a grouchy or bad mood,
his sweaters too clean,
but sometimes Bob was a little bit depressed.
He was more than just play-frustrated with *Mr. Moose,*
Bunny Rabbit and *Mr. Green Jeans.*
Bob seemed authentic.
Here was an adult that wouldn't lie to kids.

I wish I had a reason
to mention Paul Tripp's *Birthday House,*
or Officer Joe Bolton and *The Three Stooges,*
or Zacherle playing with Jello
and hosting horror movies on *Chiller Theater.*

I dreamed I was *Dead End* kid Billy Hallop
with flying suit stolen from *Commander Cody.*
My pure intentions meant rules didn't apply,
I was naïve, good, fought temptation
but Pom-Pom chocolates, *Green Lantern,*
Dr. Strange comics, *Famous Monsters,*
and *Mad Magazine* were my weaknesses.

Sometimes I believed I was the only one
who understood why
all of this was so vital.
No, not the decoder rings
and Cracker Jack box puzzles,
or even going to Paramus in Jersey
when malls were brand new.
Secrets were being told to me
through these television prophets,
even though I couldn't always decipher them.
I knew if I could only understand them

I would never be as boring or as unhappy
as my parents were.

God Bless Doris Wishman

Yes, yes
those exquisite Parisian films
Renoir, the visual poet,
the virtues of Kurosawa
bravery of Keaton
masculinity of Ford
madness of Peckinpah
grace of Lean
self-destructive genius of Welles...

Too proper, too formal, I must slip into
something more comfortable like a
double feature of *ReAnimator*
and *Jason and the Argonauts*
or a dusk till dawn marathon with
Robot Monster, Bad Girls Go to Hell,
Pink Flamingos, El Topo,
Godzilla Versus the Smog Monster,
and *Plan Nine from Outer Space.*

I envy not the obsessions or dreams
of the misguided Ed Wood, Junior,
but marvel at the faith, vision
and energy he possessed
to make something out of
less than nothing and
become immortal.
Never mind it didn't last,
that he was washed into a gutter
of sleaze and alcoholism—
he lives again, forever...
forever.

"Because all of you on earth
are idiots!"

Ron Ormond will play
his 12 string guitar
until your ears bleed and you admit
Mesa of Lost Women is like
no other movie ever made.

Doris Wishman was 90
 when she died in August 2002,
still making a movie.
…from nudie cuties to roughies,
to porn and gore,
and back to grindhouse sleaze…

Wishman, the most prolific
woman director of all time
had a vision—
a vision to keep making movies
keep trying to make better
and better movies
she relied on no one but herself.

I have visions too,
but lack the madness
that would make me risk
everything on a roll of the dice
or take a double dare leap over an
abyss that I could never
hope to jump across.

I can have false modesty and
pretend I could do better
but I don't risk everything.

I calculate the risks
And TRY
rather than just...do
because I'm not
absolutely sure,
and I want to be absolutely sure,
and I don't drink enough
to be absolutely sure.

My father taught me to have
faith in God above,
but not faith in myself.
"It's in God's hands!"

Hands I've never seen.

Yet others say:
"It's good to be in God's hands."

PRAY!

I'm not sure a dreamer
belongs there.

God bless you Doris Wishman.
God bless you.

More About Father and Son

"You'll never amount to anything!"

"Are you ever going to learn?
Are you going to sleep all day?
You can't go on like this.
You need to go to church!"

"You'll never amount to anything!"

"Don't talk back to me!
There are no free rides, pal.
You think you have it tough?
Who the hell do you think you are?
You better straighten up.
This is my house, my rules."

"You'll never amount to anything!"

"This is no way to live your life
What the hell is the matter with you?
When are you going to grow up?
Turn the music down.
What do you know about it,
Mr. Butt-inski?
Not fair?   Life isn't fair."

"You'll never amount to anything!"

"Money doesn't grow on trees.
Don't you care what people think?
Stop being so selfish.
Shut up and listen to me for a change.

You're going to wind up in jail."

"You'll never amount to anything!"

"I don't want to hear about it.
You need to be more responsible,
Mr. Smarty Pants,
Mr. Know it All!
Call me when you DON'T need anything.
GOOD BYE…"

"Hello? Is everything okay?
Where are you?
It's been too long
since we've heard from you."

"I tried to call you
but the number was disconnected.
You taking care of yourself?
Well you must be doing something right.
I don't know how you do it.
I'm proud of you!
You know you can tell me anything,
I'm here to listen.
Well, you know where we are.
I love you."

Brake

Not so fast,
not too close,
I break.

A Moment of Peace

I'm sitting with my ghosts
at a large round table.
We're having coffee and tea
and some cinnamon toast.

There's several here
I don't know at all,
missed opportunities
which aren't very clear.
There are friends I never made time for
(never even tried),
friends I completely ignored,
and friends who died too early
(before I understood much at all).

There are the lovers I never slept with
(could have, but chose not to),
the lovers I wished I slept with
(but I said or did the wrong thing
at the wrong time, ruining the slim chance I had),
the lovers I barely remember at all,
the ones I never called back, and
the lovers who gave me their trust, perhaps their hearts
and I disappointed them in ways
large and small.

No reason to say
"I'm sorry."
Too late.
And they don't want that,
that's not why they are here.

There's fear
guilt and self-doubt.
Ghosts I barely see at all
who represent
all I've forgotten
standing against the wall.

My favorite pets
are quite agile and able.
They are playing again
underneath this
large table.

I'm sitting with ghosts,
with these feelings
of people
I can never forget.
I have nothing to fear.
They aren't angry with me
and I'm not full of
melancholy or regrets.
Heck some of them
aren't even really here.

We're having cinnamon toast,
coffee and tea,
and the oddest thing
of all,
or so it seems to be,
is that my ghosts
seem so comfortable
just sitting here
with me.

The Wedding Photograph

"Let your life lightly dance on the edges of
Time like dew on the tip of a leaf."
—Rabindranath Tagore

In the wedding photograph,
my father looks barely old enough to drive
a fish out of water, too skinny,
(ears too large),
dressed in a fancy tux, extra-wide tie
big white carnation
nervously smiling
seeing blank canvas entitled
"from this day forth."

Look closer…
giant ferns in the background
of this table they share.
The wedding cake topper
out of focus in the foreground
in front of dad.

In front of mom
two candles burning.
She looks calm, poised, composed.
Her diaphanous wedding veil,
her white wedding gown,
the princess getting what she
is supposed to want.
Clean linens, champagne,
family, friends…
Her arm through his,
their hands together
just below his breast jacket pocket.

Is hers balled into a fist
his wrapped around it?

Dad knows...
but he wants
stillness, no attention on him.
She can't simply be placed
neatly into his life.

What am I doing here?
No, I mean I'm happy to be here,
People taking pictures,
so many pictures,
a fancy reception
—All this attention on us.

His marriage WILL
be happier than his parents.
He WILL avoid making the mistakes
his father made.
She is worth it.

Vaguely he knows somehow there will
be a place of their own,
soon a Master's degree in electrical engineering
and children perhaps.
He knows more than one is best.
He will give more than he ever got.

This is our glorious day
they want to be happy for us.

Happy wife,
able to look so poised and beautiful
for this picture.

Dad can't quite get comfortable
being in the spotlight.

Sixty years and more than
three thousand miles away,
their son now holds black and white
memory,
composing
revisionist words of a time
and place he never knew,
seeing Dad as an overwhelmed
young man
at the beginning
of what will define
the rest of his life.

Not a Self-Made Poem

The writer's fingers weren't
bloodied when he typed
on his keyboard
with the fury of Pete Townshend
thrashing his guitar.

Now through the pea soup fog
of self-doubt
the loser formerly known as
'you won't amount to anything'
steps up to the microphone
and reads a muted scream
filtered into a poem about
sunlight sliced by evergreen
bristles into beams of light.

The calm demeanor
never lets you even imagine
a sexually abused past—
it's been washed off his sleeve
long ago by a downpour of word play,
soothed by peppermint balms of humor
redirecting rage under titanium pan
frying up doubt and lack of confidence
that sticks to the Teflon coating
though the pretender at the microphone
ignores the irony with every breath.

Millie

The surface of the lake ripples
as cool breeze soothes
partly cloudy sky,
the perfect Northwest light, warm.
It accentuates the shades of green
my blue eyes spy.

I stand in appreciation.
How fortunate I live in this place
where a majestic view, such as this
of immense lake, green trees,
stretches out in front of me.

I can be at water's edge in five minutes.
Touch the water I am looking at,
in less than five minutes.
I can slip off my shoes
and feel the icy cool lake water,
look for mallards, ducks, blue herons.

Someone will be out in a kayak,
another in a sailboat.
I can wave to a jogger:
a teacher who taught my daughter
will bicycle by.
I can watch an elderly couple
walk slowly on dirt paths,
…in less than five minutes.

I am trying not to be too depressed.
My Aunt has just died.
It's good her suffering has ended.

My memories of Millie
are from several years ago,
not from this past year.
I didn't want her to suffer with the cancer;
no one deserves such suffering.
She who shared and gave so much
should be shown mercy and compassion.
Little could be done to help her.
Time to say goodbye.

The snapshot memories
of her at family gatherings:
smiles, a tone of voice, laughter.
The time they drove 200 miles
(we drove 50) to meet and have dinner:
warm, caring, generous.
I cut short family gatherings as teenagers often do,
later realizing the era of close families was ending.

It was not so common for so many
aunts and uncles and cousins
to gather together several times per year.
Not anymore,
not ever again.

I saw her son two years ago.
Joey still had enough of his youthful face
that I remembered
moments nearly forgotten at family gatherings.

It had been nearly three decades since I saw Joey.
He wasn't at the weddings two decades ago.
Almost one decade since I saw Aunt Millie
and Uncle Larry.
Time passes.

Ripples on the surface of the lake.
I can be there in five minutes.

600: A Poem About Baseball

In 1994 I briefly re-caught baseball fever
realizing Ken Griffey Junior is someone's
Mickey Mantle.
New to Seattle, I root for the hometown team
remembering when I was 7
and the Mick wearing my age
patted my shoulder, gave me
a signed baseball as I stood
proud with Pop-pop in the House
that Ruth built.

In 1995, the Mariners seemed to be magic:
A-Rod, Buhner, Edgar, Big Unit and Junior.
They even beat the Yankees
for division championship
playing in the funky Seattle Kingdome
full of louder
than The WHO crowd cheers, and the
wave and fireworks
and Ken Griffey hitting lots of homeruns.

600 for the Kid today! June 9th, 2008!
Now playing for Cincinnati.
The 6th baseball player to ever hit 600.
Baseball is about numbers, statistics,
percentages, averages...
Who EVER wants to be average?
Sounds horrific to be averaged?
But not to break records, hit homeruns,
take a victory lap around the bases.

Those cold confusing numbers of Math class
we hated and rebelled against
were relished when it came to baseball.
Frigid corporate business
this modern major league baseball be.
Yet so much warmth associated with it.
America's past time: Mudville,
Angels in the Outfield, Babe Ruth,
Robinson, Clemente, Gibson, Yogi Berra,
Yaz, Sammy, Rizzuto, Mickey, Harry Caray
and the Bleacher Bums,
DiMaggio, Ted Williams, Lou Gehrig,
Koufax, Maris, Cubs, Yankees,
Amazing Mets, curse of the Bambino
Red Sox, and everyone's favorite
or adopted new home town team.

I say D...
I say Dee... OH...
belted out Danny Kaye:
D—o—d—g—e—r—s.

And then I read how Griffey
played with his dad back in 1990
HITTING a home-run right after
his dad hit a homerun—
only father-son back to back home run
in professional baseball history!
Fans love that shit. I must still be a fan.

"Junior," Ken Griffey Junior, that is,
left Seattle, partly to reunite
and play with his Dad again.

Griffey Senior made 2,143 hits
during his 19 year career
and Junior got his 2,143th hit on Father's day
June 20th, 2004,
it was homerun number 500.
His dad was there watching!
You can feel how numbers become
something warm and wonderful.

My relapse into Baseball fever lasted 2 years
and I showed my daughters
how Pop-pop taught me to
score the games.
K is strike out, BB is base on balls—a walk,
6–4–3 DP is a classic double play.
Who's on second? No! He's on First,
Today's pitching, Tomorrow's catching.

I recall walking through Yankee stadium
with Pop-pop as he said Hi
to people like they were his friends,
and he would proudly announce
he was there to enjoy
another game with his grandson…
"He's a south-paw,"
he'd say.
"Might play here one day, who knows…"

No baseball player for me,
but say hey...
Junior just hit home run number 600.
Mighty Casey jumps to his feet,
tips his hat,
and I feel Pop-pop glowing with pride
as Mickey looks at him and says,
"Fine young man, there."
"Yes, sir."

Rides With Dad

I wake up at 4:00 a.m. with the kind of thought
that makes me catch my breath,
swallow hard.
I won't get back to sleep.

Two weeks ago I picked up my daughter after school
like so many times before.
I didn't mark the occasion with any special significance.
I didn't take an extra breath,
I didn't take the kind of pictures with my eyes
and brain that I would have taken
if I had thought of it as the last time
I would be doing this.

She was waiting, leaning on the wall
in the back of the school
with her too heavy back pack
and a notebook in her hand.
For me it was an errand.
Your daughter needs a ride home from school
like so many many times before—
it was a chore—a burden.
She often was not where she was supposed to be
or she was late, and sometimes
I even got angry that she made me wait.
Oh, how I hate to wait when I pick someone up.

She didn't make me wait this last time.
As I pulled the car partially into
the driveway to let her in,
she was already picking up her backpack,
moving to put it in the trunk, before quickly

slipping into the front seat.
"Hi, Dad," she said, like so many times before.
"How was your day?" I said turning the car around.
"Okay, kinda boring."

As I drove down the tree lined street,
turned around the small traffic circle
went down the hill to the busier 23rd Ave,
turned right into traffic,
I thought about what lane I wanted to be in.
Could I get around the bus
that would be stopping in a few blocks
or would I be stuck behind
someone making a left hand turn
across a busy street?
Should I let her change the radio station
to what she wanted to listen to?

"I'll do it," I said, pushing the button
to a compromise station that played music
I sometimes liked and she could somewhat enjoy.
I wasn't thinking:
This was the last time I do this with her.

Next year at this time she will be away
in college, on her own.
She won't need me to pick her up.

I know I'll look up at a clock in a few years,
it will be the time I would pick her up at school
and I will think about how I'm not late
leaving to get her

and all the times I was on time and waited
impatiently for her to show up and get in the car.
The times she ran up to the car, with excitement
to tell me something that happened.
The times she was leaning against that wall,
waiting for me.
She won't be telling me about her day at high school.
She won't ask me to explain something
or tell me about a profound thought,
or a strange dream she had.
"You ever have that kind of dream, Dad?
What do you think it means, Dad?"

Until I woke up this morning.
I missed the significance of the moments we had
a few weeks ago,
It's part of her growing up—me growing old.

We don't want to make too much
of these memories
and let them weigh us down.
We move slower every year as it is.
It would be worse to not have such thoughts, though.
It would be worse to not mark their significance.
We take a moment to realize
a chore, a sometime inconvenience
means something.
There are moments
some very good ones
that were shared
on the rides home from school.

I think of riding in the car with my father.
I wanted to make the rides better for her
than many of the ones I had with my father.
Sometimes I know our rides were better.
A few were not.

Now she'll have memories
of riding in the car with her father.
Riding in the car after school

with me.

Poughkeepsie Poem

I liked Bloomfield.

The little house and yard seemed bigger then.
The neighbors, St. Thomas school, the corner store
I bought comic books and Pom-Pom candies
with Pop-Pop's allowance money.
We were 20 minutes away from Grandparents,
Aunts, Uncles, Cousins,
family Memorial Day picnics,
badminton, kickball and softball games—
an hour from Jersey shores.

Dad was away a lot,
but that made the house quieter,
calmer.
And when he was home he wasn't angry
or upset.
Good to be home.
Home.
Bloomfield Home.
My Home.

Only they were getting ready to move.
They forgot to tell me.
Poughkeepsie New York,
76 miles, 90 some minutes away
from Bloomfield New Jersey.
Big suburban house.
Big yard.
I didn't want to go
I was happy in Bloomfield

I knew Bloomfield
I saw Terry Drugs light up
on fire one evening,
I knew the shortcuts.
Liked sledding down Snake Hill.
Had friends to play
Cowboys-and-Indians,
Hide-and-seek,
Kick-the-can,
trade comic books
flip baseball cards.

I got in trouble at school
often after the move.
I switched from St. Martin's
to Hagen Elementary, skipped
to 3rd Grade. Runt of the class.

In fourth grade,
Mr. Goldfluss had us write
letters to NBC to try and keep
Star Trek on the air.
History teacher Mr. Carter wore
a hearing aid. We pretended we
were talking, moving our mouths
and watched him adjust his hearing aid
and then shouted loudly at him.
I was always in trouble.
I hated Poughkeepsie.

Dad and I were always fighting.
He threw me out when I was 11,

I ran away the first time when I was 12
I hitched across the country at 13.
Barely showed up at school at all
my junior year,
took courses at Vassar,
ran to Los Angeles at 17.
I hated Poughkeepsie.

I visit Poughkeepsie,
not the crumbling ghetto city of Poughkeepsie,
but the prosperous town of Poughkeepsie.
And Hyde Park where Roosevelt Home
and Vanderbilt Mansion
and CIA
(as in Culinary Institute of America) reside.

The footprints of the malls I knew as a child remain,
But 'Monkey' Wards, and Bradlees
and Merits department stores are long gone.
Instead, Stop and Shop, Price Chopper, Marshall's,
even Barnes and Noble, Starbucks,
and Five Guys Hamburgers.
The old Howard Johnson's motor Inn
is a cheap motel to be
avoided now, much better is Hampton Inn
or Holiday Inn Express
just up the street.

Where was I?

Driving past a still operating Drive-in Movie theater.
I stop to take a picture of the dinosaur. Or at least the

starts-at-dusk *How to Train a Dragon 2* marquee.
Rhinebeck's Beekman Arms Hotel, established 1776.
George Washington actually did sleep here.
17 miles from Poughkeepsie.
Pete Seger's Clearwater cleaned up the
Hudson River.

IBM added over 150,000 families to
the area at its peak.
The trees have gotten bigger and greener,
the malls have expanded,
the empty lots and fields filled in with
Colonial style houses sitting on half acres of
manicured lawns.

At dusk the lightning bugs, the fireflies I never
saw in Los Angeles and don't see in Seattle
make me smile.
No, not because it's Poughkeepsie,
because they were part of Bloomfield.

I never wanted to move to Poughkeepsie.
They made me do it.
And the nearly 10 years I spent in Poughkeepsie
felt longer than the 19 I lived in Los Angeles,
and much longer than the 21 I've lived in Seattle.

They'll be selling the house
after 49 years.
Something else I notice, the last four digits
of their phone number—
1 9 4 9.

The split level, 4 bedroom, 2 bath,
brick-front house that sits on 3/4 of an acre
at the intersection of Cabin Way
and Meadow View Drive.
Although the mail box
and driveway are on Cabin Way,
Mom and Dad liked the address
17 Meadow View Drive
better than 1 Cabin Way…
and it used to confuse the post office.
There also used to be a meadow view outside,
with pheasants, geese, peacocks and
sometimes wild turkeys running around.
Houses started moving out the birds within 5 years.

If I didn't hate living there so much
I might have realized it was
a pretty good place to grow up.
Maybe I didn't want to grow up.

I feel obligated to get to know Poughkeepsie
a little better
as my 87 year old parents move
to senior apartments in Troy.

I liked Bloomfield.

My Father Should Know

I am both 57 and 7 years old
when I think of my 88 year old dad,
30 years beyond the one who
admitted imperfections
and sincerely apologized
for some of his mistakes that caused pain
to his stubborn,
on-the-other-side-of-the-country,
rebellious, runaway son.

"New book? Wow!" he might exclaim,
"You really hit it out of the park!"

No. Pure fantasy.
Dad would never use a baseball analogy.

He could barely feign interest in sports
when I played Pee-Wee league at age 8.
He would dutifully drive me to
and from games,
but he would rarely sit and watch them.
He was not a play-catch-with
his-boys sort of Dad.

He was yard-work, "I need peace, quiet,"
"no talking," and "elbows-off-the-table" Dad.

"It could have been worse," he might say,
though this too is fantasy.

He'd more likely say,
"You had it pretty good, right?"

expecting and needing me to agree with him.
And since it definitely could have been
'a lot worse',
I can offer him sincere agreement.

Hell, he's 88 and no one of his generation
was born with perfect parental skills.
There weren't even any Parenting for Dummies
books or DVDs to explain how to raise a child.
It was the 1960s—
it's a wonder either of us survived!

He's told me on the phone
he is impressed
with the person I've become.
I've received more approval
than a lot of sons will ever get.
A lot more than he ever got from his father.
He was far better to his children
than his father had been to him.

Still I worry that the poems
in my new book will make him feel
over-exposed and uncomfortable.
They might rip open some old wounds
and create new conflicts over past issues.

I don't want him to wake up
in the middle of the night
with regrets of what he didn't do.

This evolution of father and son
I write about
is part of a necessary process
I dedicate to my siblings,
my daughters,
and mom.

Dad, I'm where I am right now
because of you.
I write this
not to excuse my mistakes
by passing blame to you,
but to learn how to forgive myself
for all the time wasted
holding onto things that don't matter.

And, to let go
of all the unnecessary words
until the most important ones appear
and I can work up the courage
to simply say thank you,
I love you, Dad.
I'm blessed to be your son.

I Don't Want to Forget

"I was brought up to try to see what was wrong and right it. Since I am a writer, writing is how I right it."

—Alice Walker

I don't want to forget.

She told me the story again.
I liked hearing it anyway
and we haven't seen each other
or talked like this for 6 years.

"Your dad hates when I say it,"
she says with a chuckle and
a little repositioning of her head
that makes me realize
she genuinely enjoyed being a
little naughty, a bit of a rascal.

I must get it from her.

I'd better explain
so you'll understand the story.

My mother's maiden name is
Wright (*'W-r-i-g-h-t'*).
She once had 6 brothers and sisters.
Two are left.   She's 87.

"Oh he hates it when I say it." she says.
"Did he ever find it funny?"
"Maybe, probably not…" She says.

"As I like to say, I used to be Wright
before I got married."

Of course when you hear this,
it sounds like:
"I used to be *r-i-g-h-t* before I was married."
And if you know my Dad is an engineer,
an **IBM THINK** man
for nearly 30 years, an only child,
an A type control freak personality,
a devout catholic who later in life
became a deacon for over 20 years,
you might realize
this little act of rebellion from mom
pushed his button **HARD**
every time she uttered it.

God bless her.

What I suddenly realize this time
is how mom delivers the line with
the sort of perfect comic timing her
beloved Johnny Carson sometimes used
when delivering his Tonight Show monologues.

Henny Youngman had:
Take My Wife, …please.
Mom has: "I used to be Wright,
before I was married."

My Dad was in the hospital,
internal bleeding.

Things took a turn for the worse,
I hopped on an expensive flight
from Seattle to Newark,
rented car to Poughkeepsie.
Dad recovered, but it took a
few extra days.
We talked quite a bit in the hospital.
He was worried about Mom.

Mom had trouble walking.
She would NOT use the cane Dad got for her.
Mom hadn't left the house in over a year
and that was to attend the funeral of her sister.
Mom wouldn't go to the doctor.
Mom wouldn't permit strangers into the house.
Mom would have anxiety attacks.
Dad took care of her.

Now he was in the hospital
worried about Mom,
home alone,
going up the stairs
without anyone around.
Would the neighbors bring the papers and mail
from the driveway and mailbox to the front porch
where Mom could get them?

We talked in the hospital about many things,
most weren't important or controversial.

"How's your mom doing?" he asked me
even though he just talked to her on the phone
ten minutes before I got there.
"She seems okay.
We've had some nice conversations.
I got her lunch and then
some jelly doughnuts
from Dunkin Doughnuts."
"Oh wonderful, she loves jelly doughnuts.
I'm so glad
you are here, helping us," he says.

We joke, make witty comments
at the nurses, hospital staff,
and visiting chaplain who
came from India 30 years ago.
He really was named Charles Heston.
"Oh so that was your chariot outside
taking up two parking spaces," we joke.

Mom and dad have been together over 60 years.
"Your mother drives me crazy, you know,"
Dad reminds me for the third time in the last hour.

"And you let her," I say again.

This time he asks, "What do you mean?"

"A perfect example: Something she says,
that she knows will always upset you."

"What's that?"

"I was Wright before I was married."

"Oh I hate that," he says loudly, fists clenching.
"She used to say that to our friends
and family all the time."

"It's funny,"
"Not to me," he says.
"She knows that. That's why she still says it."
"She enjoys hurting me."
"She enjoys realizing that you can't control
 everything about her or yourself."
"What?"
"She knows how you will react when she says it.
She knows she can get one up on you
and sometimes that is a very difficult thing to do."

"Do you think she loves me?" he says
in a little quiet voice I've almost never heard before.
I don't hesitate: "There is no doubt in my mind
she loves you very much."

He says nothing for a moment, then sighs loudly,
"How do you know?"

"I can see it in her eyes when we talk about you.
The way she tells me things
like how her saying
'I was Wright before I was married'
upsets you. She loves you very much."

And tears well up in Dad's eyes.
"You don't know how much
I needed to hear this. It means so much."

"It's unconditional," I say.

"Yes," he says,
his body relaxing,
his eyes closing to nap.

Not a Poem About a Cat

1.
No, no, no!
I will not succumb to the strange malady
of writing a poem to a cat.
Some I've seen have been sublime, others cute,
but most stand begging with heart on sleeve
demanding to be petted.

I will not add sentimental whiskerlings
to the pile.

No!

2.
PEACE.

The name of my cat
was Peace.

3.
Peace was a small mixed breed playful thing,
mostly black with artistically placed white markings
particularly one on the crown of its head
that formed a V (for Vendetta) on its nose.

4.
My father disliked cats,
but after several years of pleading
my younger sisters and I got our wish
and a kitten was brought into
the house.

I chose its name.

Who didn't want
Peace?

5.
Peace grew into a
large and muscular feline,
brawling with neighborhood cats
and sometimes even dogs.
He excelled in bringing
once feathered and rodent related
creatures to our front door
in tribute to its keepers.

The frequent bloodied corpse gifts
often greeted with disgust
taught everyone to look at where
they stepped.

6.
At times Peace
seemed to truly taunt my Dad
rubbing against his leg
an act met with protest,
"Stop that, I don't like you," Dad growled.

But never did he kick...

7.
Peace slept with me,
And if he was not in my room

when I closed the door at night,
he would meow and scratch
until I let him in.

8.
When Peace was four
I left home for good
and barely spoke to Dad
for several years.
One phone call he got on the phone
to tell me Peace had died.

"I thought you should know," he began.
"You're old room is my office
and he would climb onto the desk
sniff at the books you collected
and he would meow at me, as if
asking where you were.
He slept most night on your old bed."

9.
Thirty-five years have passed
but I will not write a
sentimental or cute
tribute poem to my old friend.
No, this poem is not one for a cat.

This is written for Peace,
you see,
for who wouldn't want
that?

ENCORE

"A poem begins with a lump in the throat;
a homesickness or a love sickness.
It is a reaching-out toward expression;
an effort to find fulfillment."

—Robert Frost

Poem Starter #1,027

The teenager convinced of his worldly knowledge
proclaimed to his friends at the coffee shop:

"life would be
so much easier if we
didn't take things so personal."

Not an Ordinary Poem

Ordinary things.
Write about ordinary things,
everyday things—
so we take less of daily life
for granted
...so we take less of daily life for granted.

Write of forks spearing soggy,
spongy pancakes drowning in sticky
corn syrupy sauce in a loud busy restaurant
where a family of six overwhelm a waitress
who wishes she had stayed in college
and gotten a real job in a high rise office building
with her own desk, anything other
than being a waitress,
being pleasant to six unruly kids and their dad.

"I'm a waitress at Denny's,"
she told her father on the phone.
It was the first time they had talked
in over two years

Dad was right, she married too young
the no-good bum left her in the middle of the night.
She was sorry it upset dad so much,
but she was glad she didn't have the baby.
What would she have done with a baby on her own?
She should have never dropped out of high school,
ran away from home believing in lust and love
taking for granted they could make a decent life.
He would be loyal to her, not get drunk
or ever hit her...

But Daddy was right. Life was too hard.
He wasn't good enough for her.

Dad was sorry he got so angry,
and that he didn't send money last time she had asked.
He would send her some money,
pray for her, have everyone in the church pray for her
to keep her safe and happy.
She would be welcome to come home,
could have her old room back,
it would all be much better now.

But she was just calling to tell him, she loved him,
wasn't mad at him—any longer.
"Don't need money, not coming home,
but you could visit, Dad.
Must be lonely since Mom died.
"Please come and visit," she said.
"There's room in my apartment if you want
to stay a few days, always room for Dad."

And she remembered:
puffed up clouds moving quickly
across the blue sky,
lying in the sun on the sand
of the beach on the Jersey shore,
not Asbury Park, Wildwood maybe,
smell of pine tar boardwalk, sound of seagulls,
smell of Coppertone. She dozed off to sleep...

Six kids!
How could this have happened!
He wasn't going to have any, now there are six!

And he hated Denny's,
and soggy pancakes…and just this second
he could get up, go to his car
and drive…

Drive as far as the gas in his tank would take him
and then just disappear,
become someone else.
Someone without six kids,
someone with dirty greasy hands working on cars
in an old fashioned gas station on Route 66.
After work have a few in run-down road house.
No one would know he was once a system analyst,
once a computer geek, once a father of six kids
with a big house in the 'burbs,
S.U.V., soccer mom wife,
six kids he'd take to Denny's,
Saturday mornings as a treat.
Six   crazy,   screaming,   wild   kids.

Kids who would worry him, disappoint him,
make him proud, love him, forgive him, take care of
him.

Fill his coffee cup?

She probably didn't like being a waitress,
but he wondered if she knew how lucky she was
being a waitress—
young, a life wide open as mid-west plain,
not yet stuck in a pre-made life.

Yes, more coffee,
more life.

He'd be a better father,
better father today, better father tomorrow.
Six kids was a big responsibility
and they'd turn out to be successful and good people.
They had their whole life in front of them,
and they wouldn't have to be system analysts or
waitresses at Denny's.
His kids would be more than that.
He would make sure of it.

They'd be extraordinary,
become extraordinary people,
make extraordinary contributions to society,
and on special occasions,
for purely nostalgic reasons,
they could gather together at Denny's
eat soggy pancakes, be messy, laugh too loud -

like an ordinary family
might do.

Poem Starter #1,426

"Live your dash,"
Said the man
in the cemetery.

"Live your dash."

Why

for Jack McCarthy

In his memory
hold the hand of
fallen acquaintance,
spouse, daughter, son, friend,
drunk, addict…

Help them to their feet,
look them in their eyes,
remind them there is help.
Even when they don't believe
they can be forgiven,
tell them there is hope,
that love exists.
They are human,
they matter,
and most important
there is light—
the darkness tells us so.

The opposite of love
is doubt.

Our enemy is
fear.

Everyone
falls.

Everyone
hurts.

Everyone
forgets.

You only need to
imagine you can dance
and the music will get louder.

You only need to listen
and the words
you need to hear will be there.

Today you won't believe it
but your worst fears
will make you laugh tomorrow.

Some of you gifted with grace
carry on the powerful message.

All we share
are these brief moments in time:
if they are dark
soon comes the light,
if they are bright
reach out
for the hand of another
pull them out of their shadows,
tell them the whole truth.

If they are listening
this is what they need to hear,
if they aren't,
perhaps the next time,

perhaps the next messenger,
will be the one
to simply remind them
that all of us,
the addicts and the normies,
all do life
one day at a time.

Poem Starter Ω

If our heads weren't buried
in the sand,
we'd anticipate every kick
to the ass we endure.

Veteran Eyes

for Roy

Most were drafted.
When asked how many they killed,
few answered,
most didn't really need to know.
Their 19 year old eyes were closed.

There was heat, dust, insects,
and metal fire-fly fragments.
Awful smells, screams, sobs
and their ears were ringing from how the
silence was erased with sudden deafening chaos.

As triggers were pulled
they closed their eyes
if they were ever open at all.
They were trained to point and shoot.
Team players, nearly every single one.
Self-less preservation for their
brothers-in-arms.

He didn't close his eyes.
78 was the number
or thereabouts.
Snipers kept their eyes open,
worked with spotters, picked their targets,
and confirmed their kills.
Human drones.

Later, his eyes almost closed
because of alcohol.
He imitated a normal life.

Drugs let him pretend
to sleep
until his eyes opened to escape
what he kept seeing.

Hero, they say
with medals.
Hero, they say
in ignorance, and worse—
out of guilt and shame
for not doing more for them.
Hero, they say
with political agendas
hungry for junk food headlines—
while wearing rose-colored glasses.
Hero, they say
without listening to anything
they don't want to know about.

Heroes aren't supposed to get
so depressed that more of them
take their own lives
than were ever killed in combat duty.

Heroes shouldn't have to beg
or sleep in parks and on sidewalks
when paperwork, medical benefits,
get lost and phone calls go unanswered.

The last thing heroes want
is pity or insincerity.
Anonymity is accepted,

but they shouldn't be forgotten
because they aren't the right
rank or color
for photo opportunities.

Wars don't end when we are told they end.
For some, wars don't end at all.

His wife and children had seen enough,
they were M.I.A. for two decades.
No one else was willing to keep their
eyes open long enough to help.

When he began to stay sober,
he wrote about what he saw.
78 was the official number
(there were more,
though most don't give a hair)
and he will not forget
as history repeats itself
in the eyes of thousands more.

Drive

Behind wheel of automobile
we become rage-aholic executioners.
Our neighbors hopeless, moronic,
worthless pieces of human waste
stealing the air we are forced to share.

She drives too slow.
He never turns his damn blinker off!
She pulled out in front of me
and I had to hit my brakes,
so I wish her dead.
He suddenly decided to slow down
to make a turn without warning,
so I declare him an offspring
of an unmarried dog.

She's putting on make-up
…oh for God's sakes…
He's on his cell phone—
breaking the law,
dangerously distracted while
navigating his lethal
transportation coffin.
I suggest a place he should stick his phone,
though he doesn't hear me.

Good thing I don't have a gun
or some sort of laser that would
flip his car on its side
and get it out of my way.
Where's a cop when you need one?

Oh, there's the cop!
Yikes, better make sure I'm only going 4
miles over the limit
(—damn ticket-writing pigs).

It's not me,
it's them!
No one follows the rules of the road.
No one uses common sense!
No knows how to drive
except me!

Bitter Appetizer

Too rash,
too angry,
too soon!
Truth is better
served for dessert
and with sweets.

Poem Starter #1,306

There's no loneliness
in his eyes
when he's writing.

Explaining My Poem

Explain.
Explain poetry.
Explain your Poetry.

I could.
I could have said…
I could have said, no.

Instead:
Well I don't want to…
I don't want to be too obscure.

Connecting…
Connecting and communicating…
Connecting and communicating
are important to me.

By way of…
By way of explaining…
By way of explaining I need to tell you

"I need to tell you I admire Buster Keaton."
"You admire Buster Keaton?" She asked
"Buster Keaton, the great stone-faced comedian?"

She knew who Buster was.
Buster, the great comedian who did acrobatic stunts…
Wild Acrobatic stunts and experimented
with what the camera could do.

A stunt or gag, a fall, a cheap laugh wasn't enough…
Wasn't enough for Buster…
Wasn't enough for Buster, there had to be more.

152

He intuitively knew what the audience expected,
and gave the audience what they expected.
Gave them what they expected
with a twist of something more.

So when I write a poem…
write a poem the audience will probably like.
I try to give them something extra—a twist.

Now not all poems need…
Not all poems need something extra.
Not all poems need an extra twist.

But I'm not happy.
I'm not happy with ordinary poems…
With ordinary poems even if they work.

Ordinary poems seem too easy.
They seem too easy but of course I know…
I know poems, good poems aren't ever so easy.

And I know sometimes poems try too hard.
Try too hard to be something…
Try too hard to be something they are not.

Poetry is poetry…
is poetry for what it leaves out…
Leaves out, said Marvin Bell.

Sometimes too much is left in…
Left in a poem to explain…
To explain too much.

Extra…
Extra words unnecessary…
Extra words unnecessary, just there.

"I think…
I think," she said nodding her head.
"I think I know what you mean, now."

"Good," I said,
"Very good," I said
"Good," I said, "then please explain it to me?"

Poetry! Oh, Poetry!

For darkness restores what light cannot repair.

—Joseph Brodsky

Poetry has been my ruin
sucker punched my breath away.
Tenderly held me with
promises there would be peace
while always, in ALL WAYS
letting me know I've just begun.

Poetry:
I have much to learn
to do,
to write.

In poems it rains,
from wet mists dampening the streets
causing bare skin to glisten,
to torrential downpours that
wash away the recent past.
The best poets sometimes move
between the drops, not to stay dry,
but to choose how they feel the rain.

Poetry,
oh poetry,
I asked that you teach
more about the rain,
but you demand too much at
inconvenient times,
keep me out too late,
show me liars and phonies,
hold up mirrors forcing me to
see myself.

In Poetry there is true light,
epiphanous light beaming through clouds,
dazzling as it kaleidoscopes through thick
leaf-bearing tree branches
and transforms common
rolling hill into masterpiece of
unexpected textures and shapes,
and myriad shades of green.

And then with blinding intensity
defensive poses are sandblasted
leaving me exposed, vulnerable,
confused, half-finished.

Poetry
threw me out of careers.
You are not short-order cook, journalist,
movie-maker, comedian, actor, salesman,
marketer, stock-broker, landscape
designer, or consultant, abandon all!
You are poet!

Yes, I said,
as poetry next hid from me in
unsavory places
leaving crumbs in
awful spaces, as weak and thirsty
I stumbled in my search.

Poetry
Oh, poetry!
Beloved
poetry

156

Forsake me not.
Embrace me
as I have embraced you.
Truth me into knowing,
save me from my Ignorance,
fill me with your
knowing.

Poetry
Oh, poetry
forsake me not,
clothe me,
embrace me.
Don't let me drown
in the middle of
this endless ocean
after you have guided me
to blow up the ship...

Poetry
Oh poetry.

Poem Starter #1,628

As a word, or promise
honesty
is like an unreliable witness
to an accident.

Reaction to an Eliot Quote

"Poetry is not a turning loose of emotion,
but an escape from emotion; it is not
the expression of personality but an escape from
personality. But, of course, only those who have
personality and emotion know what it means
to want to escape from these."

—T.S. Eliot

I got this.

Fuck you, T.S.!

You are, I'll admit,
more correct than wrong
in your arrogant proclamation.

I have sat through bad poetry
at hundreds of readings.
I have written many awful poems…

but the perfect poem
is a dead thing,
and I prefer life
shouted irresponsibly
with passion and emotions
into the dark night.

Words should stir
and no one should hide
for very long from the
stirring or deny too much
that our human imperfection
is something better lost.

Poetry, like love, is messy, sentimental,
you pompous ass! (Ask Alfred!)
Go write your almost perfect poems,
Eliot.

But your boasting about this
deserves exactly what
you attempt to rise above and reject:
this crude and personal
emotional response.

Reaction to a Sandburg Quote

"Poetry is an echo asking a shadow to dance."

—Carl Sandburg

Poetry is also a howl at the moon, a mournful cry in the dark of night, a train whistle bouncing off the clouds to fill the bowl with sounds of wanderlusts, a glop of grape jelly on the floor separated forever from its soul-mate peanut-butter now praying its misery and longing will end with the compromised redemption of a dog's tongue.

Poetry is a faded bright flower just inches from getting a drink of water or attention from autumn bee, a rustling of leaves and the glorious flight of one who has broken free to free fall to the earth, a moon's beam stretching through a brief opening in clouds to shine on the fertile lands of earth it will never know.

Poetry tires of impatiently lurking at the edges waiting to touch shadows and will suddenly expose itself like rotting corpses washed out of their final resting places in a flood. It believes in the futility of both love and war and craves the action, strategic pauses and the maiming involved in both.

Yes, Carl, poetry can be an echo, but it also creates its own sounds.

Ode to Neighborhood
Independent Bookstores

Poets need bookstores,
quieter places with space for chairs
without baristas noisily grinding coffee,
or rowdy drunks
demanding more beer and well drinks.

Places where poets can stretch
and grow, recite, perform,
get ornery, protest, show-off,
preen, promote,
express dangerous ideas,
cry or share their passion,
as an audience listens,
ponders ideas,
makes connections
and absorbs different perspectives.

A place where no one is censored, arrested,
or involuntarily committed to an asylum.

We need bookstores,
where you might run into a neighbor,
an acquaintance, or a stranger
and strike up a conversation.

A place you might quickly dash into
to pick up something to read,
or spend hours browsing, dreaming,
remembering, forgetting, discovering.

On the internet
you can't smell books,

thumb through them,
feel their weight in your hand.

On the internet
you can't read the hand-written comments
scribbled into the margins,
or find a birthday greeting,
or touch an author's autograph.

On the internet
you can't stop on your way
to the cash register
to investigate a book
you've never heard of,
pick it up from the table,
pull it off the shelf,
turn its pages,
feel its texture.

On the internet
you can't pick up an old friend,
a book you once read,
nearly forgot,
and experience a flood of memories.

New books have a couple of smells
old books have many.

My favorite bookstores
aren't like hotel gift shops,
they don't have perfect lighting
and aren't in shopping malls
filled with robotic muzak.

Poets need bookstores owned
not by a corporation,
but by a person
who is quirky,
not completely polished,
older than 22 and loves books,
writers, poets, students, and scholars,
more than money.

We need bookstores with
old brick walls,
concrete floors,
a bright red couch
that seems to
swallow you when you sit in it.

We need bookstores with
a chess table in the front,
miniature rocking chairs,
stuffed toys for kids in back,
and wooden bookshelves stretching
nearly 15 feet to the ceiling,
rolling ladders.

We need bookstores
that aren't taken for granted,
forgotten until they fade away
like yesterday's headlines
exposed to bright sunshine
in the store's glass-front window.

We all need bookstores
with bells above the door
announcing our arrival,
bells
that welcome us home.

Poem Starter #1,728

Just think
someday all of this
will still not be yours.

Plank Vision

for Teresa

She wants to go to the garage sale,
look for pink flamingos.

Get up early, slip out of the house
before anyone wakes up,
be alone to search through
hand me downs, maybe find
a weathered metal sundial to hang
on the deck, rain boots that would
fit a little girl, though they are gone,
grown up into people she doesn't want
anything to do with.

Maybe she'll find that green
piano book with Chaconne and Straus's
waltzes she remembered
having a long time ago.

She's always on the lookout for a good
tablecloth or a piece of hand-made embroidery.
Someone just bought
a box of forgiveness very cheaply,
she doesn't see another one.

No need for the never-used toaster,
procured for a wedding gift
many years ago…
Nothing she doesn't already have in the drawer
full of bitterness.

Maybe a green, stained-glass ashtray
that she'd fill with

marbles and set on the coffee table
 or deck, maybe an imported Tijuana
knick-knack to keep Edgar, the wooden
painted fish from Taxco company,
on top of the entertainment center.

Most of these things displayed hold memories,
they need to be exported to strangers' homes
and forgotten.

She looks for integrity, honesty, self-respect,
something that she can be passionate about,
something that will give her peace,
even for a minute or two.

Like this antique egg-timer she just found…
Now there's something she can't live
without.

But then she squeezes my hand.
She's ready to go.

We buy nothing.

Dear Poem Owner

Sorry you weren't home.
Used the words you hid
to get inside.
Moved around things
careful not to disturb…much.
Washed some dirty words,
watered the ideas you planted
and threw the adverbs
down the garbage disposal.
Seemed the least I could do.
Thanks.

Not Aloud

Watch out for
Poetry!

It never sleeps.
It will either wait for you
to discover it
or run right over you.

It's a non-profit,
perpetually on a pledge drive
rarely grateful
or content with the status quo
limited liability entity.

Watch out for
Poetry.

If the mouths that utter it
have been silenced,
it will Howl
off tablets and pages
and no court will keep it quiet.

It has more power than any King,
denies, blasphemes and praises
God.

Watch out for
Poetry.

It conforms, revolts, creates
its own music, meanings and voice,

and when necessary
tells lies to expose truths.
When it is declared dead
it resurrects, shines brighter than
Death Valley sun,
lighting up heaven and earth,
recording the trees that
fall in the forests of the subconscious
eating your plums.

Watch out for
Poetry.

Not a Van Morrison Tribute Poem

Poets should never listen to Van Morrison
when they're trying to write—

tryin' and tryin'
to write
poetry.

They shouldn't listen to Van Morrison
when they're trying to write poetry.

Poets shouldn't fall in love
when they are trying to write—

lying and crying
to write,
to write.

They shouldn't fall in love
when they're trying to write poetry.

Poets shouldn't think too much
when they're trying,
tryin' to write,
strugglin' to write,
forcing themselves
to try and write.

Not Van Morrison,
fallin' in love,
thinking too much,
trying, struggling to write,
poetry—

they shouldn't!

I Like Dead Poets

I don't have to be nice to dead poets.

If I am bored with their poems
I can close the book and stop reading.

They
will never know.

They do not ask me
what I think of their poems.

I don't have to give a drunk dead poet
a ride home.
They won't
vomit in my car.

They don't need cab fare.
I have not been stuck with a dead poet's bill.
I have not had to make excuses
for a dead poet's behavior.

A dead poet has never stolen
a phrase, or idea from me.

I like dead poets.

Someday,
I will be
a dead poet too.

Poem Starter #1,610

There's too much
to take in.
What are you
hiding?

Uh Huh

My words must be pretty important to stand up here and recite them to you…

Uh huh…

Sometimes I listen to other words and I think, those words are put together much better than my words are put together. Maybe I really don't have any idea what I'm doing, maybe I shouldn't get up and recite my words and take time away from people who put together their words much better than the words I put together.

Uh huh…

Then I hear words that are put together much worse than the words I put together and I'm almost embarrassed for the people reciting them—except for the people who believe their words glow with a brilliance that blinds.

Uh huh…

Words from stomach, words from the heart, not screwed up too much by the brain are the ones I'm after. Not too clever, just enough to make a connection, tickle, whisper, touch.

Uh huh…

In case you think, I think, I know exactly what I'm doing, I don't. But you learn more in failing and trying then you do in not trying at all. And if you really succeed, well, what then? Do you retire? Repeat yourself over and over again?

Uh huh…

I hate the sound of my voice when I hear it played back on a tape recorder, but when I hear it as I recite, bouncing off an audience listening…I don't mind it too much.

Uh huh…

I should have ended the poem earlier, at retire. That would have been a much better place to stop, but I just had to get a little indulgent and keep going, keep pushing a little harder to try and say something that might matter.

Uh huh…

Poem Starter ∞

At both ends
are beginnings.

Hope

The fuel of prayer
fills the hearts
of those with faith.

Troubles pass,
tears dry.

Winter's dark skies
reveal the brightest of stars.

Love and laughter return
like birdsong in spring.

Now,
take my hand,
walk toward the sun,

out of the forest,
leave those shadows
fully behind you.

Poem Starter #1,110

Forgive me.
I've forgotten the simple joy
of observing
leaves
floating, spinning, falling
from the trees.

The Ballet of Leaf

Too tense
I drove 10 miles per hour too fast,
to arrive a minute sooner,
to wait 10 minutes longer
for my daughter to get out of school.

Then a driver pulled out in front of me,
drove much too slow,
made an illegal left turn,
making me miss my light.

My hands gripped the wheel tightly.
Bad drivers, lights that aren't timed right,
unpaid bills, not enough income,
too much to do
not enough time.

The wind was blowing,
the rain falling sideways.
I saw a ballet that made me laugh:

a leaf danced and twirled
like a tight rope walker
on a power line above.

Defying gravity,
the yellow brown leaf used the wind
to skitter along the wire,
somersault, electric slide.

Exactly I thought,
that's it,
precisely.

Poem Starter #1,011

Truth is in
the trees
and whispered
among the wildflowers.

Dragons

Do you
remember those days
lying on your back,
looking up at the cloud dragons
in the sky,
waiting for something to happen
to transport you
from childhood?

Remember
those crazy ideas
filling your head
turning from vivid fantasies
into impossible dreams?
Somehow you were going
to make them all come true,
because the secret to doing
anything was simply setting
your mind to do it.

It was as simple as faking the
confidence to walk over to
Cindy,
asking her
if she would like to dance.
She said: "Okay"
and in that moment you knew,
that if a popular pretty girl
like Cindy would dance with you,
well, just about anything
you could think of was surely possible.

And if all it takes to reset
this optimism,
get my dreams back,
is to lie on my back look at the clouds
and wait a while…

well…
what the hell am I waiting for?

Time to lie down and look up
at the dragons.

POEM NOTES

"Not A Poem That Rhymes" (page 8)

This was written after coming across a writer's guideline for submitting poetry to a well-known literary journal. They specifically advised poets to read the publication and not send in rhyming poetry or light verse. I found it irresistible not to compose the following and submit it. I received an appreciative response from the editor who still couldn't publish the poem, but suggested another place to send it.

"Small Circle of Brautigan" (page 21)

This poem was inspired by a Richard Brautigan true story. After a girlfriend criticized one of his poems he tried to commit himself to a mental health facility. When they wouldn't take him he threw a rock at a window and was arrested. Brautigan was born in Tacoma Wa. on January 30th 1935 in extreme poverty. He established a reputation in San Francisco, publishing his first book of poetry in 1957. On October 25, 1984, two concerned friends found his body at his Bolinas neighborhood residence. He had killed himself with a shotgun. He was 49.

"Why" (page 141)

This poem was inspired by a beloved poet from the Boston area who relocated to Seattle for the last 10 years of his life. He was active in A.A. for over 50 years, staying sober and helping and encouraging hundreds of others. Jack McCarthy became a good friend. We both preached to others the importance of open mic venues and read each other's poetry. I miss him.

"Explaining My Poem" (page 152)

I call this original form A BUSTER. It uses conversation, repetition, builds up an expectation, then surprises.

"Ode to Neighborhood Independent Bookstores" (Page 162)

A much earlier version of this poem was published in *The Beacon Hill News* in 2002 as "Ode To 'Take Another Look Books' Bookstore." Take Another Look Books was where I began curating and hosting a poetry reading (twice a month in 2001) in the Columbia City Neighborhood just a few miles southwest of downtown Seattle. The reading moved a few blocks up the street to Lottie Motts (when it was a coffee-shop) and then moved again to Bookworm Exchange in 2005 when the coffee shop became Lottie's Lounge (a bar/pub). In December of 2012 Bookworm Exchange closed its doors and ended my reading series in Columbia City after 11 years. (There's a YouTube video of the final reading: https://www.youtube.com/watch?v=BZtYbZuRNXc). I revised the 2002 poem into "Ode to Bookworm Exchange." I continue hosting and curating another series monthly at Parkplace Books in Kirkland. A brand new smaller version of the Bookworm Exchange bookstore opened about a mile away from the old location in 2014. I'll probably do a special reading book-signing there...just because.

"Dear Poem Owner," (page 169)

Selected to be displayed on 2 King County Rapid Ride buses and the Rapid Ride bus station at 3rd and Bell Street in downtown Seattle November 2014–November 2015. Thank you 4Culture and the Poetry on Buses project.

AUTHOR NOTES

The earliest poem in this book originally appeared in a little chapbook called *Poems for the Working Class* in 1983 ("The Sky"), back when I was involved in the Los Angeles poetry scene. The rest of the poems were written in the ensuing years.

I got serious about poetry when I was 12 years old and published a poem in a National magazine (*After Dark*) called "Dear Troubled Youth" (a political poem about Vietnam). I very sporadically published a few other poems over the next few decades. In 1975 I moved to Los Angeles and concentrated on writing screenplays and then became involved in various television shows, eventually working on award-winning documentaries at KCET Los Angeles, before working as a producer on programs like *Hard Copy*, *Entertainment Tonight* and many others. I also contributed to or ghost-wrote parts of several produced screenplays but returned to primarily writing novels and poetry while earning a living in sales and marketing and later as a Financial Advisor for Morgan Stanley and then Waddell and Reed.

I moved to Seattle with my ex-wife (Azi), and three daughters in 1994 and began getting involved in the very active Seattle poetry scene in late 1999. I began hosting and organizing poetry readings and events in 2001 and got involved with the Washington Poets Association and PEN which had a Washington State Chapter for several years. Many special readings, events and poetry festivals like Burning Word on Whidbey Island resulted from the combined efforts of dedicated hard-working individuals too numerous to mention by name—or more accurately, I would worry about forgetting to mention a name or two who was important and instrumental to the successful events that happened over the years. One of the Washington Poets Association's lasting achievements was the creation of a Washington State Poets Laureate Program which after years of tireless efforts finally happened in 2007 (thanks to several people but special thanks are due to Karen Bonaudi whose tireless and optimistic efforts for nearly a decade proved essential).

Poetry is important in all its various forms (spoken word, SLAM, traditional, experimental). It remains an important influence to other art forms and has a remarkable ability to heal (both poet and reader/listener). It has historically connected us to each other across geographical, political and cultural barriers. I am humbled by your interest in spending time with my quirky, often informal poetry. I hope as you read this book, you are amused, inspired and moved and believe your time is well spent.

Thank you.